Apologetics for Teens

Did Jesus Rise from the Dead?

SAINT SHENOUDA PRESS

Apologetics for Teens

Did Jesus Rise from the Dead?

Bethany Kaldas

ST SHENOUDA PRESS
SYDNEY, AUSTRALIA
2021

Apologetics for Teens: Did Jesus Rise From The Dead?
Bethany Kaldas

COPYRIGHT © 2021
St. Shenouda Press

All rights reserved. Except for brief quotations in critical publications or reviews, no part of this book may be reproduced in any manner without prior written permission from the publisher.

ST SHENOUDA PRESS
8419 Putty Rd,
Putty, NSW, 2330
Sydney, Australia

www.stshenoudapress.com

ISBN 13: 978-0-6451394-3-3

All scripture quotations, unless otherwise indicated, are taken from the New King James Version®. Copyright © 1982 by Thomas Nelson, Inc. Used by permission. All rights reserved.

Contents

Introduction	9
Evidence for the Resurrection	17
Explaining the Evidence	35
Conclusion	65
Appendices & References	69

Acknowledgement

I cannot thank my family enough for all their patience and assistance putting this together. Special thanks to Fr Antonios, whose 'Proofs of the Resurrection' talk was the foundational source of the information and structure in this book, and who lent me an endless supply of research material.

Also, a big thanks goes to the Alethia apologetics team who have established a number of meetings around this subject area (among others) and allowed for open discussion about our faith.

God bless you all and may the joy of the Resurrection always fill your lives.

INTRODUCTION

Did Jesus Rise From The Dead?

> *'The New Testament writers speak as if Christ's achievement in rising from the dead was the first event of its kind in the whole history of the universe. He is the 'first fruits,' the pioneer of life,' He has forced open a door that has been locked since the death of the first man. He has met, fought, and beaten the King of Death. Everything is different because He has done so.'*
> (C. S. Lewis, *Miracles*, ch. 16)

Over two-thousand years ago, in a garden far, far away, an angel announced the best news to ever be spoken in all of history: **Christ is risen!**

Christ's Resurrection changed everything. Suddenly, there was hope of redemption for sinners. Suddenly, our pains and troubles had purpose. Suddenly, death—humanity's greatest enemy—was less than the dirt beneath our feet. Needless to say, the Resurrection of Jesus from the dead is the foundation of all Christian belief. Without it, nothing else matters.

> 'And if Christ is not risen, then our preaching is empty and your faith is also empty.'
> (1 Corinthians 15:14)

But two-thousand years is a long time. If you're reading this, you're probably spent a bit over a decade in this world, maybe two. If you're, say, sixteen years old, two-thousand years is about one-hundred and twenty-five lifetimes away! I can't even imagine what that span of time is like. If the Resurrection happened so long ago, and was an event that seems more miraculous than almost anything else, how can we really know that it happened? How do we know it isn't just a fairy-tale, a legend passed on for generations because it gave people comfort of life beyond the grave?

If you've ever asked yourself these questions, you're definitely not alone. In fact, ever since the Resurrection is supposed to have happened, people have been questioning whether Christ really did rise from the dead.

What is Apologetics?

'Reasoned arguments or writings in justification of something, typically a theory or religious doctrine.'
(Lexico.com)

Throughout your life, you're bound to run into people who confront your faith, who have different beliefs and question yours. You can, of course, let it slide and avoid the question. This is often a wise decision—but sometimes, it is actually worth addressing the issues non-believers raise with rational arguments. Not only does it show that Christianity is not a 'blind' religion of people who don't use their brains, but it can also strengthen your own faith and maybe even change someone else's perception of God or religion.

But remember, apologetics is a defence, not an attack! We are trying to reason, to create a sense of understanding, not hostile argument for the sake of proving someone wrong. Our goal, as Christians, is not to be right but to follow the Truth, because Christ is the Truth.

'But sanctify the Lord God in your hearts, and always be ready to give a defence to everyone who asks you a reason for the hope that is in you, with meekness and fear.'
(1 Peter 3:15)

Did Jesus Rise From The Dead?

Whether you're an ancient Jew in Jerusalem, wondering if the rumours are true, or a student sitting in history class in the twenty-first century, that question on which all of Christian belief hangs is a very real concern: Did Christ really rise from the dead?

Well, one of the benefits of being one of many, many people who've asked this question is that a lot of them have already taken measures to find an answer! This book will be a brief journey through proofs of the Resurrection. We'll take a look at what kind of evidence you would need to support Jesus' rise from the dead and evaluate some common theories used to discredit the Resurrection.

If you're reading this because you have your own doubts or questions about the historicity of the Resurrection, I want to assure that that's ok. Humans are rational creatures, we use our minds to engage with the world — and with God. If your faith is genuinely being hindered by questions of logic or rationality, that's normal, even healthy. It happens to everyone at some point, and it will continue to happen about anything that matters. The fact that you're willing to ask the question means that you actually care about the answer— you care about what your faith is founded upon. And that's a good thing.

That being said, understanding the historical likelihood of the Resurrection is not the ultimate aim of your Christianity. A confidence in the logical and historical possibility of Christ's

in a nutshell

ST ATHANASIUS
On the Incarnation

Dead men cannot take effective action; their power of influence on others lasts only till the grave. Deeds and actions that energise others belong only to the living. Well, then, look at the facts in this case. The Saviour is working mightily among men, every day He is invisibly persuading numbers of people all over the world, both within and beyond the Greek-speaking world, to accept His faith and be obedient to His teaching. Can anyone, in face of this, still doubt that He has risen and lives, or rather that He is Himself the Life? Does a dead man prick the consciences of men?

Resurrection is, of course, important for a Christian, but something you need to remember is that, as a Christian, the most important thing about the Resurrection is that you experience the risen Lord in your own life. It's all well and good to know evidence and statistics about a historical event, but that isn't what will *change your life*.

Before we go on, there's one other thing you need to know. You might be reading this book because you have a non-Christian friend and you want to prove to them that Jesus really did rise from the dead so that they can become a Christian. As well-meaning as that is, nobody who honestly converts to Christianity does so because they were argued into it. Love is the only thing that ever genuinely brings someone to Christ—not evidence, not logic, not debates—just genuine Christian love. But for some people, they have experienced God's love and would be genuinely interested in following Him, if only they could get past the idea that the Resurrection is mere myth. That is when knowing the historical evidence can be helpful. It is also incredibly helpful to know for your own benefit, as a Christian. A healthy, honest scepticism has its place within faith—in fact, asking such questions and searching sincerely for answers can make your faith even stronger than it would be if you hadn't. So never be afraid to look deeper.

How to History

If we're going to treat the Resurrection as a historical event, then we must first know how to approach history in general.

I want you to imagine a scene for me: *It's a Saturday, you've woken up late in the afternoon to the delicious smell of home-baked chocolate cookies. Awesome! You make your way into the kitchen, only to find that, to your great disappointment, all the cookies have already been eaten! Now it's just a matter of finding out who did it…*

History is a lot like detective work. For both crimes and distant historical events, you must start with the question you are trying to answer. In this case: Who ate the cookies?

Once you know exactly what you're trying to discover, you can start investigating. Ask witnesses—different witnesses who haven't spoken to each other (otherwise, they might be conspiring together!), look at physical evidence, things like that.

So, let's say you ask your sister Mary, who's always been an early riser, even on weekends (what a weirdo), if she knows anything about it.

'Oh yeah,' she replies thoughtfully. 'I think I saw Josh sneaking around the kitchen after Mum finished baking...'

Just as she finishes, your older brother Peter strolls into the room. He came back from Saturday mass only a little while ago, and could not have spoken to Mary since he returned. 'Hey, I just saw Josh running around with an empty plate. What's that about?' he asks.

Ah ha! You now have two witnesses giving you separate pieces of evidence that point in the same direction. The icing on the cake (pun intended), is that when you do finally see your little brother Josh, who immediately denies any knowledge of any cookies anywhere, you spot flecks of dark brown chocolate at the corners of his lips.

Now, after you've looked at the available evidence, it's time to try and get to an answer to your original question. So, who took the cookies? Well, I think you've probably worked that out by now...

If you want to show someone that a historical event happened, that's the kind of thing you have to do.

- You ask: Did this actually happen? (Or they might do the asking for you)
- Then you look at the evidence available and give it an honest examination.

From that you can form a conclusion that both answers the question and is supported by the evidence.

This method usually works really well! It's how historians and scientists go about investigating the world. But it's really important to remember

Introduction

that, especially with distant history, the evidence can never prove that something *certainly* happened. It can get pretty close—you can have so much evidence supporting a historical event that you're 99.9999999...% sure that it did happen—but you'll never really get to 100%. At the end of the day, everything in history requires at least a little bit of faith.

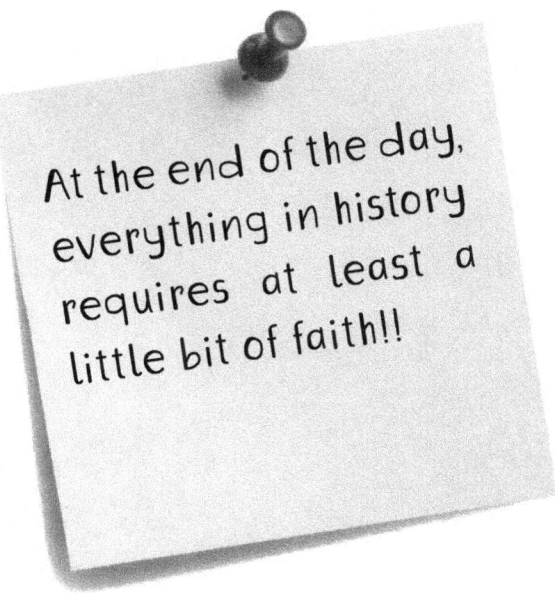

At the end of the day, everything in history requires at least a little bit of faith!!

EVIDENCE FOR THE RESURRECTION

The Existence of Christ

Before we go through the evidence for the Resurrection, it's worth addressing the question of whether Christ Himself really existed. After all, if historians have no reason to believe that Jesus was a real person, then nobody really cares if He rose from the dead or not!

We won't go into all the details about the evidence for Christ's existence (that could be a book on its own!). But as it turns out, there is very little debate among historians about whether Jesus was a real person or not.

> "We have more and earlier manuscript evidence about the person of Jesus Christ than we do anyone else in the ancient world- including Julius Caesar and Alexander the Great"
>
> DANIEL B. WALLACE, PROFESSOR OF NEW TESTAMENT STUDIES AT DALLAS THEOLOGICAL SEMINARY

Nobody seriously questions whether historical figures like Julius Caesar or Alexander the Great really existed. If we have more evidence for Jesus than we do for them, then there really isn't much doubt about whether Jesus existed.

This table compares the texts were have as evidence for the existence of the Roman emperor, Julius Caesar (who nobody really doubts exists), and Jesus Christ. Take a look and see what you think.

Evidence For The Resurrection

Source	Julius Caesar (100-44 BC)	Jesus of Nazareth (4 BC-30 AD)
Texts they wrote themselves	*Gallic and Civil Wars* (by Caesar himself)	None
Primary Sources (people who met them or lived in their time)	Cicero, Pompey, Virgil, Ovid, Cattalus, Sallust	Paul, Mark, Matthew, Luke, Peter, James, Jude, John
Recent Secondary Sources (by people who never met them but wrote relatively close to the time)	*Twelve Caesars* by Suetonius (c. 121 AD)	Extra-biblical references (texts that aren't in the Bible) -- from 52 AD onward
Later Secondary Sources	*Lives* by Plutarch (c. 105-125 AD)	Other Christian Literature — from 70CE onward
Earliest Manuscript	5th century AD	~125 AD

Note: 'Earliest manuscript' is referring to the earliest surviving physical manuscript we have as evidence for the existence of these people. There is evidence that the manuscripts we have now are actually copies of original documents that were written far earlier. For example, we have a physical text called the Rylands Papyrus now, which is a snippet of the Gospel of John. That particular document has been dated to around 125 AD, but it is believed that it is just a copy of the original Gospel of John, which is thought to have been written around 96 AD.)

Did Jesus Rise From The Dead?

As you can see, Jesus has way more primary sources about him than Caesar does! Plus heaps of other literature from after His time, while Caesar only has about two. The evidence for the existence of Jesus as a real person is overwhelming! And if we have (comparatively) so little evidence for someone like Julius Caesar—who pretty much everyone agrees was a real person who did the things that were written about him—then we should be even more confident that Christ was real and likely did the things those texts (such as those found in the Bible) say that He did.

in a nutshell

BART EHRMAN

"With respect to Jesus, we have numerous, independent accounts of his life in the sources lying behind the Gospels (and the writings of Paul) — sources that originated in Jesus' native tongue Aramaic and that can be dated to within just a year or two of his life (before the religion moved to convert pagans in droves). Historical sources like that are is pretty astounding for an ancient figure of any kind. Moreover, we have relatively extensive writings from one first-century author, Paul, who acquired his information within a couple of years of Jesus' life and who actually knew, first hand, Jesus' closest disciple Peter and his own brother James. If Jesus did not exist, you would think his brother would know it."

It's worth noting that Bart Ehrman is a *non-Christian* New Testament Scholar—and yet even he admits that Jesus existed as a real, historical figure. Of course, that doesn't mean that Jesus was God—as an non-Christian, you can reasonably believe that Jesus was a real person without agreeing that He is God, as the Christians say He is. But the fact that even a non-believer is willing to agree that Christ existed as a person means that it's pretty much undeniable.

Biblical Texts as Evidence

As Christians, we take the Bible to be a single whole, a spiritual text that must be read and lived in the context of its entirety and the whole life of the Church. But from a historical perspective, it is in fact multiple different texts. The different books in the Bible have different human authors and were written at different times in different cultures, and this means they all count as separate pieces of evidence. Having different authors who never met each other writing about the same thing generally makes it more likely for that thing to be true.

Let's take a look at a concrete example of this in the Bible by comparing the Gospel of Matthew and the first epistle of Paul to the church in Corinth:

Author and Reference	Text
Matthew 28:1-8 Author: Matthew Date: a little after 70 AD	Now after the Sabbath, as the first *day* of the week began to dawn, Mary Magdalene and the other Mary came to see the tomb. And behold, there was a great earthquake; for an angel of the Lord descended from heaven, and came and rolled back the stone from the door, and sat on it. His countenance was like lightning, and his clothing as white as snow. And the guards shook for fear of him, and became like dead *men*. But the angel answered and said to the women, "Do not be afraid, for I know that you seek Jesus who was crucified. *He is not here; for He is risen, as He said. Come, see the place where the Lord lay.* And go quickly and tell His disciples that He is risen from the dead, and indeed He is going before you into Galilee; there you will see Him. Behold, I have told you." So they went out quickly from the tomb with fear and great joy, and ran to bring His disciples word.
1 Corinthians 15:12-19 Author: Paul Date: ~55 AD	Now if Christ is preached that *He has been raised from the dead*, how do some among you say that there is no resurrection of the dead? But if there is no resurrection of the dead, then Christ is not risen. And if Christ is not risen, then our preaching *is* empty and your faith *is* also empty. Yes, and we are found false witnesses of God, because <u>we have</u> *testified of God that He raised up Christ,* whom He did not raise up—if in fact the dead do not rise. For if *the* dead do not rise, then Christ is not risen. *And if Christ is not risen, your faith is futile; you are still in your sins!* Then also those who have fallen asleep in Christ have perished. If in this life only we have hope in Christ, we are of all men the most pitiable.

As you can see, both these texts talk about Christ rising from the dead. Matthew was one of the Twelve who followed Jesus during His ministry, and the Gospel contains many stories that he was presumably present for, or at least alive for. Unlike Paul, he actually gives an account of how people discovered the empty tomb and how they came to the conclusion that Christ rose from the dead, so it does not seem that he is copying Paul.

Paul, on the other hand, did not meet Christ before His death, and is actually writing this letter about fifteen years before Matthew wrote his Gospel, so it is impossible for Paul to be copying Matthew. In fact, Paul's letters were written before any of the Gospel accounts (including the earliest, which is Mark, written around 70AD), so he could not have been copying those texts.

So, it seems highly unlikely that one of these writers copied the other, meaning they count as two pieces of evidence rather than just one.

See Appendix 3: Historical Significance of 1 Corinthians 15 for more information.

The second things to keep in mind about using Biblical accounts as evidence is the possibility that there are details in some accounts that conflict the details in other accounts. Even though each Biblical account is internally consistent, it might trouble some people to see that they don't always seem to agree with each other about some details.

As a really simple example, take a look at these accounts of what is assumed to be the same event by both Mark and Matthew:

Reference	Account
Mark 10:46 Author: Mark Date: a little before 70 AD	Now they came to Jericho. As He went out of Jericho with His disciples and a great multitude, *blind Bartimaeus, the son of Timaeus, sat by the road begging.*
Matthew 20:30 Author: Matthew Date: a little after 70 AD	And behold, *two blind men sitting by the road,* when they heard that Jesus was passing by, cried out, saying, "Have mercy on us, O Lord, Son of David!"

So you might ask: How many blind men did Jesus heal on the way to Jericho? Was it just one, like Mark said? Or is Matthew right, and there was two?

You might say that Mark just didn't bother mentioning the second blind man, or maybe these two accounts are actually of different events. Maybe one time, Jesus healed Bartimaeus, and on another journey, He healed these two other blind men.

But really, my question would be… How much does it matter?

Someone might try to argue that if two accounts of the same event have conflicting details, then they're both wrong. But in history, that's not how it works. Human memory is flawed, little details are likely to get mixed up over time—even really short amounts of time! For example, do you remember what you ate for breakfast last Tuesday? I didn't think so.

St John Chrysostom points out that little disagreements among Biblical accounts actually strengthen their validity:

> 'For if they had agreed in all things exactly even to time, and place, and to the very words, none of our enemies would have believed but that they had met together, and had written what they wrote by some human compact; because such entire agreement as this comes not of simplicity. But now even that discordance which seems to exist in little matters delivers them from all suspicion, and speaks clearly in behalf of the character of the writers.'
> (John Chrysostom, Homily 1 on Matthew)

From a historical perspective, if two people agree—word-for-word—about something that happened, it becomes more likely that they conspired together to make it up. If they disagree on little details, because their memory isn't perfect and they didn't talk to each other about the event, then that actually makes those accounts more believable.

Chrysostom then goes on to make a very important point—no matter what little differences there are between Gospel accounts, they all agree on the really important stuff:

in a nutshell

St John Chyrostom

'But if there be anything touching times or places, which they have related differently, this nothing injures the truth of what they have said. And these things too, so far as God shall enable us, we will endeavour, as we proceed, to point out; requiring you, together with what we have mentioned, to observe, that in the chief heads, those which constitute our life and furnish out our doctrine, nowhere is any of them found to have disagreed, no not ever so little.

But what are these points? Such as follow: That God became man, that He wrought miracles, that He was crucified, that He was buried, that He rose again, that He ascended, that He will judge, that He has given commandments tending to salvation, that He has brought in a law not contrary to the Old Testament, that He is a Son, that He is only-begotten, that He is a true Son, that He is of the same substance with the Father, and as many things as are like these; for touching these we shall find that there is in them a full agreement.'

It's a little wordy, but basically all Chrysostom is saying is that, although there may be little differences in Biblical accounts, they all agree on the core beliefs of Christianity: that Jesus is God and Man, that He performed miracles, died, rose, ascended, etc... All Biblical accounts will agree with these points, and that's what really matters.

The Three Keys

In this book, we'll take a look at three key pieces of evidence for the Resurrection:

1. **The Empty Tomb**
2. **The Appearances of the Risen Christ**
3. **The Confidence of Early Christians**

These three pieces of evidence were chosen because they're critical to figuring out whether the Resurrection was a historical event or not. Think about it: if the tomb was not empty, and Jesus' body was still in there, then the He could not have risen from the dead. If Christ is still dead, then nobody would have seen Him walking and talking after He was crucified. And if it turns out that the early Christians didn't really believe that Jesus rose from the dead, if they weren't very confident in the reality of the Resurrection, then we would have good reason to doubt that it actually happened.

But if all these three bits of evidence come together, if they turn out to be true, you would have really strong, logical reasons for believing that the Resurrection really happened. There may be other explanations for the evidence, but establishing that these three keys are true is an essential first step in showing that the Resurrection is a historical event.

So first, let's take a look at how historical these keys are—what evidence do we have for them?

Key One: The Empty Tomb

This is probably the most important key of all of them. It would be pretty hard to argue that the Resurrection is true if Christ's tomb wasn't empty! If someone had found the dead body of Jesus in there, there's almost no way He resurrected, and that would be a very hard challenge for Christians to face—if we could face it at all. So let's see what evidence there is that, three days after Christ's death, the tomb He was laid in was found empty.

Embarrassing Witnesses

The next bit of evidence that the tomb was empty may come as a surprise to you, but it is really important: the Gospel accounts suggest that the first people to see the empty tomb were women.

You might be asking, why is this evidence? What difference does it make if the first people to see the empty tomb were men or women?

Well, that's a very healthy attitude to have now, but back when the Gospels were being written, in ancient Jewish culture, the evidence provided by a woman was considered way less reliable than that of a man.

> *'Any evidence which a woman [gives] is not valid (to offer), also they are not valid to offer. This is equivalent to saying that one who is Rabbinically accounted a robber is qualified to give the same evidence as a woman.'*
> (Talmud, Rosh Hashannah 1.8)

For the first time ever, this blatantly sexist attitude (which none of you should agree with, mind you!) actually gives us an advantage here. In history, there is something called the 'criterion of embarrassment', which basically says that if an account is embarrassing in some way to the author, it's less likely to be a lie—because if you were going to make something up, why would you invent something that would embarrass yourself?

The fact that the Gospel accounts state that women were the first to see the empty tomb actually makes those accounts less likely to be a lie. Think about it: if you were going to make up a story about Christ's tomb being empty, wouldn't you want to say that the first

THE CRITERION OF EMBARRASSMENT

In history, you can usually consider an event more likely to have occurred if something embarrassing was admitted.

Consider, I'd be far more likely to believe that Josh had stolen the cookies if Peter had told me he saw it while he was skipping school. Peter would be putting himself at risk by making that admission, so it seems far less likely that he would be lying about it.

witnesses were reliable? Wouldn't you say that they were a governor, or a soldier, or at least a man (remembering that, at the time, the witness of a man counted far more than that of a woman)? But the Gospel writers chose to mention that the first witnesses were Mary Magdalene and other women, knowing full well that people didn't believe the testimony of women as easily as that of a man. The only real reason the writers would have done this is, well, if it actually happened that way!

So, the fact that it would be embarrassing to admit that women were the first people to see the empty tomb actually helps to prove that the tomb was empty, because if the Gospel writers had been lying, they would've written a less embarrassing lie.

The Jewish Excuses

The last reason we think the tomb was almost certainly empty is because the ancient Jews themselves (who did not believe that Christ rose from the dead!) didn't deny that the tomb was empty—they only made excuses for why it was empty.

> 'Now while they were going, behold, some of the guard came into the city and reported to the chief priests all the things that had happened. When they had assembled with the elders and consulted together, they gave a large sum of money to the soldiers, saying, **"Tell them, 'His disciples came at night and stole Him away while we slept.'** And if this comes to the governor's ears, we will appease him and make you secure." So they took the money and did as they were instructed; and this saying is commonly reported among the Jews until this day.'
> (Matthew 28:11-15)

At the end of the day, it doesn't look like anyone in the ancient world didn't believe that Jesus' tomb was empty. They disagreed plenty about why it was empty—and we'll get into some of those explanations later—but they all agreed that the tomb was empty at the time. Of course, if the tomb wasn't empty, it would be pretty easy for them to simply go and see for themselves! It wasn't far—it was in Jerusalem. It wouldn't have been hard to visit the tomb and check, which is probably why none of the ancient Jews tried to claim that Jesus' body was still in the tomb.

It's kind of funny, how at the time these excuses the Jews made were meant to prove that Christ did not rise from the dead, but now they are helping to do the opposite!

in a nutshell

> 'It would have been impossible for Christianity to get off the ground in Jerusalem if the body had still been in the tomb. His enemies in the Jewish leadership and Roman government would only have had to exhume the corpse and publicly display it for the hoax to be shattered. Not only are Jewish, Roman, and all other writings absent of such an account, but there is a total silence from Christianity's critics who would have jumped at evidence of this sort'
>
> (HABERMAS, G. R., & LICONA, M. R. (2004). THE CASE FOR THE RESURRECTION OF JESUS. KREGEL PUBLICATIONS, P. 70.)

Key Two: The Appearances of Christ

Few critical scholars reject the notion that, after Jesus' death, the early Christians had real experiences of some sort.
Gary Robert Habermas (2005) p. 149. – New Testament Scholar and Historian

Now, on to the second key piece of evidence: the appearances of the risen Christ. It's pretty obvious to say that, if Christ was still dead, even if He wasn't in the tomb, you wouldn't see him walking around and talking to people. So, the appearances of Christ after His death play a big part in showing that that He did actually rise from the dead.

Evidence For The Resurrection

But before we go on, it's important to realise that the evidence here doesn't actually prove that these people saw the risen Christ—it just shows that they believed that they saw Him. There could very well be other explanations for that (such as hallucinations), but we'll get into those details later. For now, let's see what evidence there is that people witnessed Christ alive after His death.

Biblical Texts

Like with the empty tomb, there are a variety of accounts of people seeing Christ alive after His death in the Bible, and they all count as separate pieces of evidence.

Text	Account
Acts 13:29-31 Author: Luke Date: 75-85 AD	Now when they had fulfilled all that was written concerning Him, they took Him down from the tree and laid Him in a tomb. But God raised Him from the dead. *He was seen for many days by those who came up with Him from Galilee to Jerusalem, who are His witnesses to the people.*
Mark 16:9, 12, 14 Author: Mark Date: before 70 AD	Now when He rose early on the first day of the week, *He appeared first to Mary Magdalene*, out of whom He had cast seven demons. After that, *He appeared in another form to two of them as they walked and went into the country.* Later *He appeared to the eleven as they sat at the table*; and He rebuked their unbelief and hardness of heart, because they did not believe those who had seen Him after He had risen.
1 Corinthians 15:3-7 Author: Paul Date: ~55 AD	For I delivered to you first of all that which I also received: that Christ died for our sins according to the Scriptures, and that He was buried, and that He rose again the third day according to the Scriptures, and that *He was seen by Cephas, then by the twelve*. After that *He was seen by over five hundred brethren at once, of whom the greater part remain to the present*, but some have fallen asleep. *After that He was seen by James, then by all the apostles.* Then last of all *He was seen by me also*, as by one born out of due time.

That passage from 1 Corinthians is especially interesting, for two reasons:

- It mentions a large group of people seeing Christ at the same time (v. 6)
- It mentions one of the enemies of Christ (that is, Paul, the author of the text) seeing Him (v. 8)

The first is important to note because, first of all, it's far less likely that a group of five hundred people would all be hallucinating the same thing at the same time. Second of all, Paul mentions something really important: 'the greater part remain to the present'. What he means is that most of those five hundred witnesses are still alive at the time he is writing this. Why does he mention that? Because if you don't want to take his word for it, you can go and ask them! If Paul was lying, and those five hundred people never actually saw Jesus after His resurrection, then it would've been really easy to prove, simply by going and asking the people who supposedly saw Him.

The second is important because Paul was originally an enemy of the early Christians. Remember, Saint Paul used to be Saul and played a big role in persecuting the Church, as you see in Acts 8 and 9:

> '³As for Saul, he made havoc of the church, entering every house, and dragging off men and women, committing them to prison.'
> (Acts 8:3)

> 'Then Saul, still breathing threats and murder against the disciples of the Lord, went to the high priest ²and asked letters from him to the synagogues of Damascus, so that if he found any who were of the Way, whether men or women, he might bring them bound to Jerusalem.'
> (Acts 9:1-2)

That's more than a little grudge he's holding against the Christians—he hated Christ and the Church about as much as anyone could! He was willing to do a lot to ensure that the Christians were publicly humiliated and killed, in the hopes that fewer people would follow them. The last thing he would've wanted to do is provide evidence that Christi really did rise from the dead. And yet, we have Paul himself claiming that the risen Jesus appeared to him—a claim he never would have made if he did not believe it himself.

Overall, from a historical perspective, there's enough evidence to say that the early Christians did at least believe that they saw Christ after His death.

in a nutshell

N.T. WRIGHT

'The empty tomb and appearances have a historical probability so high as to be virtually certain, like the death of Augustus in A.D. 14 or the fall of Jerusalem in A.D. 70'

See Appendix 3: Historical Significance of 1 Corinthians 15 for more information.

KEY THREE: THE CONFIDENCE OF THE CHRISTIANS

The third and final piece of key evidence we'll be looking at for the Resurrection of Christ is the confidence of the early Christians in the Resurrection.

I want you to ask yourself: How much would you go through for a lie? You might tell lots of people about it, you might even travel to different places in the hopes of convincing people to believe something that isn't true. But if you were threatened with imprisonment, torture or death for proclaiming something you didn't believe in, would you still say that you believed it?

Let's look at a little example to demonstrate the point: Stephanie is trying to convince her friends that she can fly. She can't show it to them now, because her powers don't work while other people are looking, but she got to school that day by flying there!

…She knows that what she's saying isn't true, but some of the younger kids believe it, so she keeps telling other students about it. Until her teacher tells her that if she keeps spreading that lie, she'll get suspended and will get in big trouble with her parents! After hearing that, Stephanie immediately admits that she was lying and she can't really fly (as much as she would like to).

In our little example with Stephanie, there's an easy explanation for why she was lying about being able to fly. She was getting admiration from the other kids in her school, and maybe she was even trying to use her new popularity to get sweets from her peers or something along those lines. Stephanie clearly benefited from the lie she told—that's why she told it.

Some people claim that the early Christians were doing the same thing—that they spread lies about Jesus rising from the dead to get attention, or maybe to get a lot of people to follow them. Cult leaders have been known to lie to people to gain followers and grow in popularity too—we don't say that their religion is more likely to be true because of how confident those cult leaders seem. But there are huge differences in how a greedy cult leader behaves and how the apostles behaved. For one thing, the apostles weren't benefitting from their popularity—it was getting them a lot of harassment, death threats, and eventually actual death for most of them. Where a cult leader would get featured in the news and would usually squeeze their followers for as much money as they could give, the apostles got swords and stones in the face. Not fun. And not worth it for a lie they didn't believe.

People are very unlikely to stick with a claim they know to be false if doing so would mean bad consequences for them. If the early Christians really didn't believe that Christ rose from the dead, we would expect that, as soon as they were threatened with torture or death, they would've admitted they were lying. But what do we see of these early Christians?

Evidence For The Resurrection

> *'86 years have I have served Him, and He has done me no wrong.*
> *How can I blaspheme my King and my Saviour?'*
> Polycarp's Martyrdom (~69AD- 155AD)

Just as one example of many, the martyrdom of Polycarp, although difficult to date exactly, is believed to be the earliest authentic account of a Christian martyrdom outside the New Testament. The full account is certainly worth reading for your own benefit, but for our purposes today, it's really important to realise just how confident Polycarp is in Christ. He has absolutely no reservations about being killed for the sake of his Saviour (burned alive, to be more specific), fully believing that dying for Christ would mean rising with Him. And again, Polycarp is just one of countless martyrs who believed the same.

From Stephen to modern day martyrs, countless Christians have been willing to sacrifice their lives for the sake of the risen Christ. Again, this does not prove that Christ did rise from the dead (although it was enough proof for St Athanasius), but it does provide strong evidence that the early Christians really did believe that Christ rose from the dead, enough so to die for that fact.

Explaining The Evidence

Introduction

Now let's say you've gone through these three key pieces of evidence for the Resurrection, and that's enough to show, with significant confidence, that the tomb was empty, that people really did believe that they saw Christ after His death, and that the early Christians really did believe that Jesus rose from the dead. That all seems reasonable enough to some people. But you or your non-believing friend may need more than that. After all, evidence can mean lots of different things.

Think about it: If I see some large, clawed footprints in the sand of my local beach, everyone might agree that they're real, but not everyone will agree on what that means. I might think that the footprints mean that there was a really big dog on the beach, while my more imaginative friend might think that there's some kind of coastal monster on the loose. A more sceptical person might say that a human made the footprints using some strangely shaped shoes and they're only trying to trick people into thinking there's a monster on the beach.

Finding evidence for something is only half the work—you then have to be able to show that your hypothesis is the best one to explain what the evidence means. So in this next section, we're going to take a look at five main types of hypothesis that someone might propose to explain the three key bits of evidence we've just talked about. The five kinds of hypothesis are:

> ### What is a Hypothesis?
>
> 'an idea used to account for a situation or justify a course of action.'
> (Lexico.com)
>
> For the purposes of this book, I'll be using the words hypothesis and theory interchangeably.

1. The Far-Fetched Hypotheses
2. The Psychological Hypotheses
3. The Deception Hypotheses
4. The Narrative Hypotheses
5. The Real Resurrection Hypothesis

Explaining The Evidence

We'll go through each of these kinds of hypothesis, why you might believe them, and whether they really explain the three key pieces of evidence for the Resurrection. In theory, the best hypothesis will be the one that can explain all three bits of evidence without having any major drawbacks.

This is because, if you remember, those three keys were the really relevant pieces of evidence to the Resurrection. We've established that all of them are almost certainly true—the tomb was empty, many people did believe they saw Christ after His death, and the early Christians were confident enough in His resurrection to die for its sake. We are no longer arguing about whether those things are true. That means that the ideal theory—the one that we're looking for to tell us what is really likely to have happened those two-thousand or so years ago—has to be a theory that explains all three of those pieces of evidence and has no major drawbacks that stop it from being a good theory. If a theory doesn't explain one or more of the keys, or if it has a huge problem with it apart from those keys, we can't say that it's a good theory to explain the Resurrection.

So what's the list we've got to check?

1. **Empty tomb**
2. **Christ's appearances**
3. **Confidence of the Christians**
4. **No major drawbacks**

Now that we know what we're looking for, let's begin!

#1: Far-Fetched Hypotheses

The first set of hypotheses we will call the 'far-fetched' hypotheses, and they all claim that we've gotten something wrong about the story of Christ's death and resurrection.

For example, the **Swoon Hypothesis** claims that Christ didn't actually die—He appeared to be dead, but really he only fainted. Some have even claimed that Jesus had one of His disciples—Luke, the doctor—drug Him so that it would like He died. After that, He would be able to wake up in the tomb alive and—well, still badly injured, but definitely alive.

There are a couple of reasons you might agree with this theory. First, the amount of time Jesus stayed on the cross was apparently quite short compared to most crucified adults of His health. From the Gospel accounts, we gather that Christ was only on the cross for about six hours. Crucifixions were generally known to have lasted several days depending on the health of the victim. Even Pilate, in the Gospel of Mark, seems surprised that He has already died:

> 'Pilate **marvelled that He was already dead;** and summoning the centurion, he asked him if He had been dead for some time.'
> (Mark 15:44)

Given the unusually short amount of time He spent on the cross, you might be tempted to think that maybe He did survive. And obviously, if Christ never died, then He could not have risen from the dead! If this were true, it would pose a big problem for Christianity.

But of course, as thinking, reasonable Christians, we can't simply say that because it doesn't fit with the Bible or our theology, it can't be true—we need real reasons to disagree with this hypothesis. And don't worry, there are plenty. Let's run through that checklist of ours and see how the Swoon Hypothesis holds up.

Swoon Hypothesis

The Empty Tomb — The Swoon Hypothesis could explain the empty tomb—but it would be a bit of a stretch. Remember, if Jesus really wasn't killed on the cross, He was still horrifically wounded and hadn't eaten or drunk anything for three days while the tomb was sealed. There was no way He was breaking out of that tomb on His own, so He would've needed help. Someone would've had to have opened the tomb from the outside, without getting spotted by any of His enemies (including the soldiers who were stationed right outside the tomb), to let Jesus out. Technically possible, but very difficult.

Christ's Appearances — This one is a lot easier to explain—if Jesus really didn't die, and had somehow managed to get out of the tomb, it would've been easy for Him to appear to people afterwards because He would be... well, alive.

The Confidence of Christians — It could be argued that, as long as they saw Christ after He supposedly died, the Christians would still be confident in His resurrection, perhaps enough so to die for Him. But this only works if they were really convinced He had died in the first place—if there had been any doubt in their minds, then the first thing they would've thought upon seeing Him alive is way more likely to be that He hadn't really died, rather than that He had risen from the dead.

Any Major Drawbacks? — Yes! From a medical perspective, it is highly unlikely that anyone could've survived the sort of torturous ordeal Christ endured on the cross.

> 'Josephus tells of how he had three acquaintances who had been crucified removed from their crosses, but **despite the best medical attention two of three died anyway** (Life 75:420-21). **The extent of Jesus' tortures was such that He could never have survived the crucifixion and entombment.** The suggestion that a man so critically wounded then went on to appear to the disciples on various occasions in Jerusalem and Galilee is pure fantasy.'
> (William Lain Craig (2010) p. 252)

> 'Thus, it remains unsettled whether Jesus died of cardiac rupture or of cardiorespiratory failure. However, the important feature may be not how he died but rather whether he died. **Clearly, the weight of historical and medical evidence indicates that Jesus was dead before the wound to his side was inflicted and supports the traditional view that the spear, thrust between his right ribs, probably perforated not only the right lung but also the pericardium and heart and thereby ensured his death ... Accordingly, interpretations based on the assumption that Jesus did not die on the cross appear to be at odds with modern medical knowledge.'**
> (Edwards, W. D. (1986). On the Physical Death of Jesus Christ. JAMA : The Journal of the American Medical Association, 255(11), 1455–1463.)

Another major drawback to this theory is that the Roman soldiers who attended crucifixions were not permitted to leave the scene before ensuring the victims were dead.

> "The attending Roman guards could leave the site only after the victim had died, and were known to precipitate death by means of deliberate fracturing of the tibia and/or fibula, spear stab wounds into the heart, sharp blows to the front of the chest, or a smoking fire built at the foot of the cross to asphyxiate the victim."
> (Retief FP & Cilliers L, 2003)

We see in the Gospels that the legs of the two thieves who were crucified with Jesus had their legs broken, and this is likely to kill the victim by suffocation within minutes. Jesus Himself had the spear to the chest, and the large flow of blood and water from his side showed that His heart had been punctured, as well as the cavity of fluid around his heart and lungs. The soldiers who did this were no new at it—they had killed crucifixion victims before. They know how to recognise when someone is dead and how to ensure that they do die even if they aren't sure. And they always had to make sure they got it right, because if they accidentally let a victim live, it was really bad news for them!

So although the Swoon Hypothesis does it's best to explain the three key pieces of evidence, it's explanation of the third key (the confidence of the Christians) is not terribly strong, and overall, the theory has a huge drawback that makes it near-impossible.

There are a couple of other hypotheses that fit in to the category of 'far-fetched'. Let's take a look at the two more hypotheses of this type and see if they do any better than the Swoon Hypothesis.

The next hypothesis is the **Wrong Tomb Hypothesis**. The idea of this one is that the disciples simply went to the wrong tomb and that's why they didn't find Christ's body there. It's an... interesting idea. Let's see how it matches up to the evidence:

Wrong Tomb Hypothesis

The Empty Tomb — This theory is trying to explain the empty tomb—after all, if the disciples (and the Marys, and everyone else who bothered to check) went to the wrong tomb, then the tomb they went to by accident could have been empty. It's not impossible, but we will soon discuss why it's very close to being impossible.

Christ's Appearances — Going to the wrong tomb and finding it empty would not explain why people saw Jesus after His death. If they went to the wrong tomb, and His dead body was still lying in the tomb of Joseph of Arimathea, then why are people seeing Him alive?

The Confidence of Christians	Perhaps the disciples went to the wrong tomb and began to preach that Christ is risen because they didn't see His body there. But if I were someone listening to them at the time, I would want confirmation that the tomb was actually empty before I could stake my life on that fact. And if it really was the wrong tomb, then that is not confirmation I would get. So no, the Wrong Tomb can't really account for the confidence of the Christians. rom the dead.
Any Major Drawbacks?	Yes! And it's pretty obvious—how could anyone make a mistake that big?! And even if they did, why would nobody check?!

The Wrong Tomb would (maybe) explain the empty tomb, but explains pretty much nothing else. And it doesn't even really explain the empty tomb. Think about it: Joseph of Arimathea—the man who buried Jesus—put Christ's body in *his own tomb,* and it is highly unlikely he would forget where his own tomb was! Similarly, Mary Magdalene and the other women saw where Christ had been buried, making it extremely unlikely that they would go to the wrong tomb after that.

Not only that, but if anyone ever questioned whether Christ was risen at the time, there was nothing stopping them from simply *going to the right tomb* and checking for themselves! And once someone found Jesus' body exactly where it had been left—in Joseph's tomb—word would have spread that the disciples were wrong and that would've been the end of it. But remember what we said about the empty tomb? Even the enemies of Christ at the time never denied that the tomb was empty—they only ever tried to explain why it was empty. But they would have been certain about which tomb Jesus had been buried in, and they, like everyone else, knew that the right tomb was empty. So no, the Wrong Tomb is clearly not the theory we are looking for.

The final far-fetched hypothesis is perhaps the most bizarre of them all—the **Twin Hypothesis**. Some people have actually said that it was not Jesus Himself who was crucified, but His identical twin who died in His place. Or, that Jesus was crucified, but His twin went around and pretended to be Him after His death.

Strange? Yes, very. But before we dismiss it, let's see what the evidence has to say about this theory:

TWIN HYPOTHESIS

The Empty Tomb — If Jesus (or His twin) were crucified, then His body would still be in the tomb, regardless of whether He had a brother or not. The only way this could work is if someone stole Jesus' body, but alone, the Twin Hypothesis doesn't really account for why the tomb was empty.

Christ's Appearances — Twin theories were designed to account for this. If Jesus (or His twin) had been crucified and He was still alive, then He could go around and pretend to be the same Jesus who was killed on the cross. But even this is a bit of a stretch—after all, it's very likely that the people who had served with Christ for three years would be able to tell the difference. It also would not explain the print of the nails or the wound in His side which Christ's disciples saw and felt after His resurrection (if the brother had not actually been crucified, how could he have holes in his hands, feet and chest?). So, although the Twin Hypothesis tries to account for Christ's appearances, it does a very poor job at it.

The Confidence of Christians	For the general masses, like the five hundred who saw Him all at once, maybe the Twin Hypothesis could explain why Christians were so confident that Jesus had risen. But think about a close friend of Christ's, like Thomas, who would not believe that the Man he saw was Jesus until he felt the wounds in His hands and side. It is unlikely that the disciples would have been fooled enough to die for the sake of an imposter.
Any Major Drawbacks?	Yes—I'm sure you know it already. We have no reason at all to believe that Jesus had a twin. It's never mentioned in any account about Jesus, Biblical or otherwise—including the account of Christ's birth, which would have included the birth of two boys if there had been twins.

Well, we've given the Twin Hypothesis a fair go, I'd say, but it accounts for pretty much nothing. You are now welcome to dismiss it.

At this point, I think it's safe to say that the Far-Fetched Hypotheses are not great explanations for the evidence we have. Perhaps the next theory will do a better job?

#2: Psychological Hypotheses

The next group of hypotheses are all to do with perception and the minds of the people involved. It could be that the people who saw Jesus after He died were only imagining that they saw Him, but He wasn't really there. Or perhaps

Keywords

<u>Hallucination:</u> a sensory (like seeing, or feeling, or smelling, or touching) experience of something that isn't really there.

<u>Delusion:</u> an unchanging belief in something that is not true.

<u>Mass hysteria:</u> irrational beliefs or behaviours by a group of people.

they were all deluded, holding onto a belief that could not possibly be true in the face of evidence that He was dead. For these psychological hypotheses (such as hallucination, delusion or mass hysteria) to be true, there it would mean that most of the people who came into contact with Christ would have had some kind of mental illness that made them see Him when He wasn't really there.

Let's take a look at our checklist and see how well this theory fits.

Psychological Hypotheses

The Empty Tomb Right off the bat, psychological explanations of the evidence do not account for the tomb being empty. It's one thing to say that the people who saw Christ were imagining Him being there, but if He really wasn't there, then He should still be dead in the tomb! As mentioned before, the tomb was easy to access—people could just check to see if He was there!

Christ's Appearances This theory was designed to explain the appearances of Christ. And initially, it does seem like a plausible explanation: the followers of Jesus were heartbroken after His death, it would not be surprising if they imagined He was there or deluded themselves into believing they had seen Him when they had not. But remember that passage from 1 Corinthians 15? The one that said that about five hundred people saw the risen Christ at the same time? Mass hallucinations, as far as modern science is concerned, don't really happen—*five hundred* people simply do not all hallucinate the same thing at the same time!

The Confidence of Christians Arguments could be made either way about the confidence of the Christians. If they are delusional, then they would be dead certain that Christ is risen, and willing to do anything for it. If it was a mere hallucination, it would be reasonable to think that they would've questioned their experiences of the living Christ.

Any Major Drawbacks? Yes! There is no other evidence to suggest that the people who saw Christ had mental illnesses that would cause such consistent hallucinations or delusions—they never hallucinated anything else or behaved in a way that suggested they were mentally unstable. Not only that, but you need to be under certain conditions to hallucinate. We all know that drugs or being extremely hungry or thirsty could potentially bring on hallucination, but there's no reason to believe that this is what was happening to those who witnessed Christ's appearances. If you're not experiencing any of those extreme circumstances, then you have to be in a certain state of mind to hallucinate something like this. Usually, you have to be in a state of expectancy—if, for example, the disciples were really expecting to see the risen Christ, then it might make a hallucination more plausible. This just isn't the case though—the disciples were heartbroken after Christ's death, they were despairing and certainly were not expecting to see Him again (especially when you consider those like Thomas or James who were real sceptics). They definitely weren't in the right state of mind to hallucinate Christ's appearances.

It doesn't look too good for the psychological hypotheses. Whether it's hallucination, delusion or mass hysteria, these theories do not account for the empty tomb (which, as we've mentioned before, is incredibly important evidence of the Resurrection), and has a significant drawback. Overall, it doesn't account for the evidence well and just seems very unlikely.

But what if it wasn't something as innocent as delusion or hallucination? What if someone was spreading lies about Christ's resurrection on purpose? Next, we'll take a look at the Deception Hypothesis.

#3: Deception Hypotheses

Of all the theories we've looked at so far, this is probably one of the ones you are most likely to hear. We've already said that it's unlikely that the disciples and all those other people hallucinated or imagined they saw Jesus after His death… but what if they were making it up? As said before, cult leaders have been known to spread lies quite convincingly in order to keep their followers. Perhaps that's all the disciples were doing. Or maybe they just didn't want to look bad.

Well, the Jews of the time who opposed Christ certainly thought that the disciples were being deceptive. Remember, they wanted to say that Jesus' followers had stolen His body to trick everyone into thinking that Christ rose from the dead. But let's put this theory against our checklist and see how well it goes.

Disciples' Deception Hypothesis

The Empty Tomb Deception could explain the empty tomb—though it wouldn't be easy. It would mean that the disciples somehow took the body from the tomb, which was not only guarded but also blocked by a stone that was incredibly difficult to move. The apologist, William Lane Craig, has observed that in modern debates about the Resurrection, almost nobody argues that that Christ's body was stolen, since it's simply too implausible. The alternative option is that Christ didn't actually die and someone let Him out of the tomb, like in Swoon Theory, but as we've said before, that's really hard to believe.

Christ's Appearances For this to work, not only would the disciples have to be lying, but also the crowd of five hundred people who saw Him all at once. To say that all of those people were lying about it is not impossible, but it's beginning to sound a lot like a crazy conspiracy theory! An alternative option is that the disciples staged an elaborate event to make it look like Jesus was alive—like, they hired an actor who looked a lot like Him and told him exactly what to say and how to act to trick people into thinking he was Jesus. It's...not impossible. And it's not unprecedented (in those times, it wasn't unknown for people to pretend to be, say, emperors who had died in order to try and convince people they were still alive). If anyone remembers, people did the same thing with Elvis Presley not too long ago. But in any of these cases, the deception was discovered at some point—none of those tricks was ever believed for over two thousand years! So it's possible, but incredibly unlikely.

The Confidence of Christians	This theory has a lot of trouble explaining this. It's the same principle behind the criterion of embarrassment (go to the section on **Embarrassing Witnesses** if you want a refresher on that)—people are way less likely to stick to a lie if it will cost them a lot. Of the twelve disciples of Christ who all preached that Jesus rose from the dead, only *one* of them was not martyred for his preaching. Not to mention all the tortures and painful deaths other early Christians went through for preaching that Christ rose from the dead. If they were all lying about it, why would they be willing to go through so much for the sake of that belief? They would have gained nothing from it.
Any Major Drawbacks?	Other than what has already been said, there actually aren't many major drawbacks to this theory. One could argue that it's unlikely since it seems out of character for the disciples of Christ to lie so persistently, but that's pretty speculative. Honestly, deception theories don't need any more major drawbacks—they're already pretty flimsy to begin with!

There is another form of deception hypothesis that some people find a bit more convincing. What if it wasn't the disciples doing the lying—what if someone was tricking the disciples? Plot twist! Let's see how this theory holds up.

DECEIVED DISCIPLES HYPOTHESIS

The Empty Tomb — This explains the empty tomb in exactly the same way as the first kind of deception hypothesis, except it would be some other group of people stealing the body instead of the disciples. As noted before, this theory of explaining the empty tomb doesn't really amount to much.

Christ's Appearances — Again, this pretty much goes the same way as it did in the previous version of the theory, but it would mean that someone else was tricking the disciples into believing that they were seeing Jesus after He died. This would probably need an actor or a lookalike, and as I said before, that wasn't unheard of in those times. But now you have an extra problem—the disciples knew Jesus really well while He was alive, it would be incredibly difficult for someone to trick them into believing that an actor was actually Him, especially given the intimate conversations the disciples had with Christ after His Resurrection. So, it isn't impossible, but it's very hard to believe.

The Confidence of Christians — This version of the theory can explain the confidence of the Christians a little better. Let's say the disciples really believe that the pretend Jesus is actually Christ risen from the dead, and they believe all the lies they've been fed—they might be very confident in His resurrection then, perhaps enough so to die. The people who know that it's all a lie may never have been faced with the threat of death because of the lie they spread—they may not even have been Christian. So this kind of deception theory actually does kind of account for the confidence of the Christians (although it would be really hard to convince the disciples of that lie in the first place).

Explaining The Evidence

Any Major Drawbacks?	There's one main drawback to this version of the theory that the first one doesn't have—why? Just... why? What would anyone gain from convincing Jesus' disciples that He rose from the dead? It's not that there isn't an answer to this question—maybe there is a reason someone would do this—but it's very hard to imagine what reason that might be and that makes it rather difficult to believe.

The deception hypotheses aren't looking very convincing, are they? It's a big stretch for mere lying to explain the empty tomb, and trying to explain the appearances of the living Christ after His crucifixion sound a bit whacky. And as for the confidence of the Christians, deception makes no sense on the first version of the theory. Who would be willing to die for something they knew was a lie? And although the second version of the theory goes a little better with the third piece of evidence, it goes way worse with the second piece of evidence: how could you deceive the disciples—who lived and worked with Jesus for three years!—that this imposter was actually Him? Overall, deception theories don't explain the evidence very well.

#4: Narrative Hypotheses

Narrative hypotheses are a little complicated, so we won't go into too much detail—but it is good to know what the arguments are trying to say and why it doesn't hold up well. There are two main kinds of Narrative Hypothesis I'll be looking at here, let's call them the **Chinese Whisper Hypothesis** and the **Myth Hypothesis**.

The **Chinese Whisper Hypothesis** argues that there was a bit of truth in the story of Jesus, but the miraculous parts of the story got added on later. So, maybe there really was a Man named Jesus, and maybe He taught that people should love each other, and maybe He was killed on a cross. But let's say that was all He was, and that was all His disciples ever thought of Him. This theory says that it was only later that people started adding things to the story—like that Jesus claimed to be God and that He performed miracles and rose from the dead. It would all be nothing but a story that grew way out of control.

It's like a game of Chinese whispers. Think of it as something like this:

A sad disciple is really cut about Jesus' death, and he starts to talk about Christ really passionately, saying things like, 'It's like He is still with us!'.

Let's say a random fisherman overhears this and tells his fellow fisherman, 'Did you hear what that disciple of Jesus just said? He thinks Jesus is still with him!'

That fisherman then goes and tells his wife, 'Have you heard? The disciples of Jesus of Nazareth believe Jesus is alive!'

His wife then tells her friend, 'Can you believe it?! Jesus of Nazareth is still alive! He rose from the dead!'

Now, that's definitely not an accurate description of how it would've happened, but you get the general idea. See how that first statement got misinterpreted, and then the misinterpretation was misinterpreted, and then again—until the meaning was completely changed? The first version of narrative theory says that's kind of what happened—maybe people misinterpreted the words of the disciples, and eventually the whole thing blew up into a ridiculous story about Jesus rising from the dead!

It's a bit of a weird one, but let's see how it matches up to the evidence.

Chinese Whisper Hypothesis

The Empty Tomb Well, this theory does not at all account for the empty tomb, mainly because (and I know we've said this a few times but it keeps coming up), if anyone wanted to disprove the narrative that Jesus rose from the dead, all they'd have to do is check the tomb! If it was all just a story, a rumour gone wild, then the tomb definitely shouldn't be empty.

Christ's Appearances	Again, this theory can't really do much to explain the appearances. Maybe if the only accounts of Jesus' post-death appearances were long after the actual event, you could say that people got so used to the story that they might've mistaken someone else for being the risen Christ. But most of Jesus' appearances happen right after His supposed resurrection. **See Appendix 3: Historical Significance of 1 Corinthians 15 for more information on how early the accounts of the Resurrection were.**
The Confidence of Christians	The argument here would be that the early Christians heard the false story of Jesus' resurrection and that was enough to get them to sacrifice their comfort and even their lives for Him. This argument doesn't really hold though, because Christians were being martyred for the sake of the risen Christ long before a story like that would've had time to develop. Stephen for instance, one of the earliest Christian martyrs we know of, was thought to have died somewhere between 33-36 AD, which is less than a decade (only a few months, or perhaps a few years, at most) after Christ Himself would have risen! That's not enough time for Chinese Whispers to twist the story of Christ's death into one of a Resurrection.
Any Major Drawbacks?	Yes! One of the main ones being that there really wasn't enough time for the story to change so drastically—something like that should've taken many generations. And if it did happen really quickly, then people were still able to check at the tomb to see if it was true! The Jews especially would've had strong motivation to produce the body of Jesus as soon as such a rumour showed up—if Christ was still dead and they indeed had the body. But let's look at this in more detail.

This is one of the most important things to realise is that many of the accounts of the Resurrection were actually written really, really close to the event itself! Remember this passage from Paul's writings:

> *'For I delivered to you first of all that which I also received: that Christ died for our sins according to the Scriptures, and that He was buried, and that He rose again the third day according to the Scriptures, and that He was seen by Cephas, then by the twelve. After that He was seen by over five hundred brethren at once, of whom the greater part remain to the present, but some have fallen asleep. After that He was seen by James, then by all the apostles.'*
> (1 Corinthians 15:3-7)

Historically, this passage has been dated to, at most, only about twenty years after the Resurrection would have occurred! And historians believe that what Paul was writing in this letter was actually a sort of Christian creed that had been passed on to him by other Christians when he converted—which means that the belief that Christ is risen is even older than that letter! That certainly doesn't leave a lot of time between Jesus' death and the appearance of that creed, not enough time for the story to change so much. Not only that, but the people who witnessed Christ's death were still alive—if they didn't believe Christ had risen, they would have protested against the claim that He had!

> *'The earliest evidence we have for the resurrection almost certainly goes back to the time immediately after the resurrection event is alleged to have taken place. This is the evidence contained in the early sermons in the Acts of the Apostles.'*
> (John Drane, quoted in Habermas (2005) p. 143.)

As a comparison, we do actually have some made up accounts of the Resurrection. Now, if someone was going to tell a fake story about how Jesus rose from the dead, this is more like how it would sound:

> *' And in the night in which the Lord's day was drawing on, as the soldiers kept guard two by two in a watch, there was a great voice in the heaven; and they saw the heavens opened, and two*

> men descend from thence with great light and approach the tomb. And that stone which was put at the door rolled of itself and made way in part; and the tomb was opened, and both the young men entered in.
>
> When therefore those soldiers saw it, they awakened the centurion and the elders; for they too were hard by keeping guard. And, as they declared what things they had seen, again they see **three men come forth from the tomb, and two of them supporting one, and a cross following them: and of the two the head reached unto the heaven, but the head of him that was led by them overpassed the heavens.** And they heard a voice from the heavens, saying, Thou hast preached to them that sleep. **And a response was heard from the cross, Yea.**'

Giant Jesus and a walking, talking cross—now that's how you write a story! That is a passage from the supposed 'Gospel of Peter'. You've probably never heard of it before, and if you're flicking through your Bible right now you won't find it. For one thing, it was written way after the synoptic Gospels—at around 150-200 AD, and appears to have been written to support a heretical view at the time known as the Gnostic heresy, which claimed that Jesus did not rise physically (hence his absurd enormousness). If you wanted to write a legendary account of the Resurrection of your Saviour, surely this is how you would do it! The vastly more reliable Gospels (Matthew, Mark, Luke and John) take on a far more realistic approach, containing all the embarrassing details (as we mentioned earlier).

So, the whole idea of a Narrative Hypothesis might seem a little ridiculous at this point. You might be wondering why anyone would even think of it. But this theory gets more gravity when you realise that the idea of a god dying and then rising from the dead is not unique to Christianity. It's actually a trope found in a lot of mythologies all around the world.

Now let's take a look at the second Narrative Hypothesis: the Myth Hypothesis.

As mentioned before, in mythologies all around the world, there is usually at least one story of a deity or divine figure who dies and then comes back from death or the underworld. Christ's resurrection follows the same pattern: Jesus, God on Earth, is killed, goes down into Hades, and then rises from the dead.

This kind of story is in Egyptian mythology, with Osiris and Baldr in Norse mythology. It's also seen with Ishtar in Mesopotamian myth and Persephone in Greek myth, who die and rise regularly every year! There are many more.

A lot of these 'dying and rising gods' are thought to have come about as an explanation or reflection of agricultural or seasonal cycles. People saw that plants—especially their crops—withered and flourished regularly, and may have used the death and resurrection of a fertility deity to explain why that happened (as in the case of Persephone and Demeter in Greek myths).

To some, this is proof against Christianity. If a god dying and rising from the dead is common in so many different stories, and we don't seem to think any of those myths are true, why do we think that the Christian version of the story should be any truer?

Well, again, let's see how this matches up to the three key pieces of evidence we have.

Myth Hypothesis

The Empty Tomb This version of the theory suffers from the same flaws the Chinese Whispers Hypothesis does. It has no explanation for why the tomb was actually empty if Jesus' resurrection was only a story imitating pagan myths.

Christ's Appearances	And once again, like the first narrative theory, this one can't explain Jesus' appearances very well. Most of the appearances are said to have happened almost immediately after the Resurrection itself, and the accounts would have been easy to verify by simply asking the people who had supposedly seen Him alive. Therefore, any myth of His appearances would have been easy to refute simply by asking the witnesses.
The Confidence of Christians	This has the same problems as the Chinese Whispers theory. Martyrs for the risen Christ existed long before a myth about the Resurrection should have had time to spring up, and even if such a legend did come about quite soon after the event, it would have been easy to disprove. If it was so easily disproved, by either asking witnesses or just checking whether the tomb was empty or not, then it is unlikely that anyone would have risked their lives for belief in something that had been shown to be untrue.
Any Major Drawbacks?	Well yes—at least three, which I'll go through in more detail below. It is important to know what this theory has gotten wrong, because although it might sound weird to you, it's a more popular view than you'd think.

Let's take a look at the main problems with this argument, and some solutions to the apparent problem of Jesus' story looking so similar to other pagan legends.

1. ***Similarity does not mean impossibility***

The fact that a certain story is reoccurring in lots of different cultures doesn't mean none of them are true. In fact, it would be a little weird if all these different cultures—many of which had no contact with each other—came up with the same plotline and there was no truth to the story at all. Wouldn't it be more likely that they were all drawing from something they all saw was true, and changed it to fit their own circumstances?

Let me give you an example to make this idea a little clearer.

Imagine that there is a really old mountain that people have been living at the base of for generations. The earliest inhabitants of that area have stories that a great dragon lives at the peak, and that you can see it flying at night. Later on, some travellers claimed they saw a vast bird flying over the mountains during the day. A madwoman once proclaimed that there was an alien spaceship on the top of the mountain—she saw something huge flying around the peak! In modern times, most people believe that it was a flock of bats.

Now, from all those different reports, it might be difficult to say what exactly the thing flying over the mountain is. But however you try to explain the flying thing—it would be very strange to claim that, because many people thought there was something flying over the mountain and they can't agree on what it is, there is therefore nothing flying over the mountain!

In the same way, it would be really weird to claim that, because lots of different cultures came up with a similar story in their myths, that proves that all of them are wrong. It's far more likely that they were all seeing the same thing (in some way), and just couldn't agree on what it really was.

2. **Same same, but different**

The second issue with using pagan myths as a reason to doubt the Christian Resurrection is that most of the pagan stories that really closely resemble Christ's death and resurrection were actually written well after the establishment of Christianity. Baldr, from Norse myth, is probably the most common example people use, since his death and resurrection really does resemble Jesus' very closely. But, although Baldr as a Norse god is quite old, that story was only written after Christians came to the pagans and had converted a lot of them to Christianity. The reason Baldr's story looks so much like Christ's is because it was written to look like Christ's! It wasn't the Christians copying a pagan story—it was the other way around.

When you look at the older dying and rising god myths—the ones from before Christ's incarnation, like Osiris, Persephone and Ishtar—the resemblances aren't even that great anyway. If the Christians had just copied a set of old pagan myths, you would expect them to be more similar. But take a look at all these differences:

- Christ died voluntarily (none of the other gods did that)
- Christ died for the sake of others, out of love (none of the other gods did that)
- Christ only died and rose once (Persephone and Ishtar die and rise every year)
- Christ was not only God, but also Man (none of the other gods were human)
- Christ's death (the death itself, not just the Resurrection) was a victory, not a defeat (for all the other gods, their death was something tragic)

So, although the basic structure of having a divine entity die and then rise again is present in a lot of stories, the Christian story is significantly different! Even if the pattern is there, the Christians clearly weren't just copying old myths they'd read. Christ's story is something new in a very real sense.

3. **Myth became fact**

Finally—and this is the big point—there is no historical evidence at all that any of the other gods really existed. But as we've already said, Christ's existence as a real person here on Earth is almost undeniable by any serious historian—Christian or not. Even if there is some resemblance between Christ's dying and rising and those of old pagan gods, the fact that Christ is real and the other gods are not is a pretty big deal! And the reality of Christ makes all the difference.

> 'The Divine light, we are told, 'lighteneth every man'. We should, therefore, expect to find in the imagination of great pagan

> *teachers and myth-makers some glimpse of that theme which we believe to be the very plot of the whole cosmic story--the theme of incarnation, death and re-birth.* **And the differences between the Pagan Christs (Balder, Osiris, etc.) and Pagan stories are all about someone dying and rising, either every year, or else nobody knows where and nobody knows when. The Christian story is about a historical personage whose execution can be dated pretty accurately, under a named Roman magistrate, and with whom the society that He founded is in a continuous relation down to the present day.** *It is not the difference between falsehood and truth. It is the difference between a real event on the one hand and dim dreams or premonitions of that same event on the other.'*
> (C. S. Lewis, They Asked for a Paper, ch. 9)

That quote was a bit complicated, so let me break it down: C. S. Lewis is saying that, if the eternal truth is that God became Man and died and rose from the dead, we shouldn't be surprised that other people, before Christ's incarnation, recognised this eternal truth and tried to show it in their own stories. They're like reverse echoes of an event that comes after them. But the big difference is that those other stories never physically took place—they were what people imagined that eternal truth might look like—but they never happened in history. Christ is different in a very important way—Christ actually is God Who became Man, and He really did die and rise from the dead (or at least, that's what we're trying to show in this book).

So even the resemblances that do exist between Christ's story and those of the myths are not a problem for us. All those legends point towards something that really did happen, in the real world with real people at a known time and location. Christ is the truest fulfilment of all those stories the ancient people told, with none of the distortions they added to it. In Christ's actual death and resurrection, not only did He bring together Heaven and Earth, but also Story and Reality.

Explaining The Evidence

> *'God sent the human race what I call good dreams: I mean those queer stories scattered all throughout heathen religions about a god who dies and comes to life again, and by his death has somehow given new life to men.'*
> (C. S. Lewis, *Mere Christianity*, bk 2, ch. 3)

#5: The Real Resurrection Hypothesis

We've looked at a lot of theories trying to explain the evidence at hand. And so far none of them have done a really good job at it, whether it's because they don't explain one or more pieces of key evidence or because they have some major drawback that makes the hypothesis unbelievable. But there is one hypothesis we haven't considered yet, one that won't even occur to some people.

What if the Resurrection really did happen? What if the accounts that this wonderworking Jew came back alive after being brutally murdered on a cross are true? Of course, we chose those three key pieces of evidence because they are relevant to the Resurrection and will determine whether the Resurrection is a historical possibility. Any theory would have to account for them to explain the Resurrection, so let's see how this theory holds up.

Real Resurrection Hypothesis

The Empty Tomb	The real Resurrection explains this perfectly, because if He is risen, then there is no dead body in the tomb.
Christ's Appearances	Again, if Christ really did come back from death, then that completely explains how people saw Him after His death.
The Confidence of Christians	Christ's actual resurrection and interaction with the early Christians after His death explains completely their confidence in His resurrection and willingness to die rather than deny it.
Any Major Drawbacks?	Well, there's just one—but it's a big one that, for a lot of people, cannot be accepted: the Resurrection is a miracle.

After looking at all of these options, it would be reason to come to the conclusion that the only actual reason not to believe that Christ rose from the dead is that such an event breaks the natural laws of science. The laws we know of our world say that once a living thing has died, it stays dead—especially if it's been dead for three days! Whether you're a Christian or not, you have to admit that the Resurrection is a miracle.

So the only question to answer now is: are miracles possible?

Miracles

By definition, a miracle is something that defies the laws of nature we know through science. So, it's no wonder that people might be sceptical when they hear about one—and even more so when they read about one in a document that's about two thousand years old.

Some people have argued that science gives us a complete picture of the universe—our theories tell us facts about the world and there is nothing in the world that goes beyond them. But if you're a good scientist, you know that isn't the case.

> ### What is a Miracle?
>
> 'An extraordinary and welcome event that is not explicable by natural or scientific laws and is therefore attributed to a divine agency.'
> (Lexico.com)

For one thing, science never gives you facts—they're called theories for a reason. Scientific models and theories will tell you about patterns that are usually seen in the world. Something like Newton's Laws of Motion will tell you that if I kick a soccer ball it should roll in the same direction as my foot's impact point. But there is nothing certain about it—it is not a fact, even though people used to think that it was. And in fact, Newton's Laws don't apply in every situation (Einstein's theories showed that if you are travelling near the speed of light or near a black hole, Newton's Laws fall apart).

Explaining The Evidence

So if you know that science tells you patterns that can possibly be broken, at least, by other scientific laws, then you cannot begin by assuming that they cannot be broken by something beyond science too. The only way you'd be able to prove for certain that miracles are impossible would be to examine every single instance in the universe, across all of time and space, and show that none of them broke the laws of nature.

It's like, if you wanted to prove that there are no black swans—that black swans are impossible—then you would have to look at all the swans that ever lived and ever will live and show that none of them are black.

Of course, this does not prove for certain that the Resurrection happened. It does not prove that a miracle occurred. But what this does mean, is that it is not logical to deny the possibility of the Resurrection purely because it is a miracle and you don't think miracles can happen.

Conclusion?

Whether the Resurrection of Christ really happened or not is an important question, especially for the Christian. If we are to have any hope, if Christianity is to have any meaning, the Resurrection cannot just be a metaphor or a legend. There needs to have been a real Jesus who really did die and who really did come back to life.

A lot of people think that Christianity is a blind belief, that we leave our brains at the door of the church and refuse to think for ourselves. But that couldn't be further from the truth! A diligent Christian is willing to honestly look at the evidence available and come to a conclusion about what that evidence means. If the evidence shows that we believe something that cannot be true, then we should be humble enough to admit it. But I hope that after reading this book, you realise that the evidence does quite the opposite in the case of the Resurrection.

Just as a short refresher, we looked at how history works and what it means for evidence to support a theory. Then we looked specifically at evidence is relevant the Resurrection. Any theory about the Resurrection would have to explain these bits of evidence. Remember the three keys?

- **The empty tomb**
- **Christ's appearances**
- **The confidence of the Christians**

Those three keys are pretty much undeniable historically—even non-Christian historians will agree that they're almost certainly true. But there are plenty of different theories out there that try to explain them. Some of them are a little whacky (really, Christ had a twin nobody knew about?), while others need to be considered more carefully. It's important to know what each of these theories is actually trying to say so that you can see if there are any problems with them. And it turns out that there are a lot of problems with most of them!

If you're trying to defend the faith, you need to do it rationally, honestly. People won't listen to what you have to say if you try to trick them into believing in God, or if you refuse to look at the evidence at hand.

Conclusion

Apologetics means defending the faith with reason and logic, not avoiding difficult questions.

For some people, searching for answers to these questions isn't so pressing. You might be content to have a living relationship with the risen Christ, and that is enough evidence for you (and something important for all Christians to have regardless!). For the Christian, dwelling in the life of the risen Christ, being changed every day by His love, and showing that love to others, is vastly more important to our faith than historical investigation.

But it's important to know that there is a strong historical, rational foundation for our faith. For some people, it can be hard to have a strong faith in something that you don't really know much about. If you are investigating your beliefs honestly (that means not avoiding hard questions and not asking even harder ones for the sake of being troublesome, but out of genuine curiosity) then you are genuinely seeking the Truth. And isn't that one of the main goals of a Christian?

> 'Jesus said to him, "I am the way, the truth, and the life. No one comes to the Father except through Me.'
> (John 14:6)

What you've learned here is not that the Resurrection definitely happened. No evidence could ever prove, without any doubt, that any event in history happened—especially one so long ago. There will always be a little question mark about anything in the past.

But this book should show you that the Resurrection is very, very well-supported by the evidence we have available to us. If you or anyone you know was trying to argue that the Resurrection was just completely made up and had no historical basis, all this evidence shows otherwise.

I hope this has shown you that Christians don't have to leave their brains at the door to believe in such wonderful things as Jesus rising from the dead. In fact, Christianity has always been firmly founded on reason—logic does not contradict faith, it can actually make it stronger. And as the Resurrection is the core of our entire Christian life, we can rest easy knowing that we believe something that history agrees with.

As I mentioned before, none of this is certain. We can't definitively prove, with historical or scientific evidence, that the Resurrection is real, any more than we can prove that Caesar or Alexander the Great were real. But we're lucky, because unlike Caesar and Alexander, there is a way for us to be even more confident in the Resurrection than we ever could be in any of those other historical events or figures. That is by meeting the risen Christ, every day of our lives.

The evidence has opened the door—history and logic are no barriers to us—and when you do step through that door, He is the one who awaits you on the other side.

> '*I am the door. If anyone enters by Me, he will be saved, and will go in and out and find pasture.*'
> *(John 10:9)*

APPENDIX 1: Faith and Reason

The question of whether the Resurrection is a historical event is one of reason. It seems like an objective question, which means that there is an answer to it that doesn't depend on what anyone thinks or believes. It's a question more like 'Did the sun rise this morning?' than it is, 'What does the sun mean to me?'

Questions of reason are resolved by looking at evidence—that's what historical and scientific investigation is. You look at the evidence in front of you, and from that, you try to draw a conclusion about the answer. And with both science and history, if the evidence points to an answer you didn't expect or one that you did not previously believe, you are supposed to put aside your earlier beliefs in favour of what the evidence is telling you.

Think about it like this: imagine you've grown up your whole life being taught that there is a monster living in your cupboard. One day, you finally get up the guts to open your cupboard and—surprise!—there's no monster there! Reason says that, based on the evidence (the lack of monsters in your cupboard) you should change your mind, and no longer believe that there is a monster in your cupboard.

That's a bit of an oversimplification, but you get the gist. Reason is based on evidence, and what the evidence tells you should shape your beliefs.

Faith seems to be a different story. To a lot of people, faith means believing something regardless of what the evidence tells you. It's like this: if you have faith that there is a monster living in your cupboard, then even if you look inside and see no monster, you'll still believe that there is a monster living there.

There are some non-Christians (and even some Christians!) who believe that this is how we approach God. No matter what the evidence says, a Christian will still believe that Jesus died and rose from the dead. Even if there was a body in the tomb that turned out to be Jesus. Even if we had proof that Jesus never appeared to people after His death. Even if there was no evidence that the early Christians were confident in the Resurrection. If we had evidence against the Resurrection (like Jesus' dead body, for example), then it would be unreasonable to believe that He rose from the dead.

Because it looks like reason is belief *because* of evidence and faith is belief *despite* evidence, a lot of people think that you can't have both. A lot of people assume that this means a faithful Christian has to ignore evidence and abandon reason in order to be a Christian at all.

However, for the Christian, faith doesn't mean quite what other people think it means. It certainly doesn't mean leaving your brain at the door of the church and blindly believing everything a priest or teacher tells you! Believe it or not, you can be a Christian while having both faith and reason. They don't need to conflict.

> ## ABSENCE OF EVIDENCE IS NOT EVIDENCE OF ABSENCE
>
> Put simply, a lack of evidence for something doesn't count as evidence that something doesn't exist/isn't true.
>
> If we had no evidence for the Resurrection, that's still a very different thing to us having evidence against the Resurrection.
>
> As it so happens, we actually have evidence for the Resurrection, which is an even stronger case.

> 'Faith and reason *are like two wings on which the human spirit rises to the* contemplation of truth; and God has placed in the human heart a desire to know the truth- in a word, to know himself- so that, by knowing and loving God, men and women may also come to the fullness of truth about themselves.'
> (Pope John Paul II)

> '**I call him truly learned who brings everything to bear on the truth**; *so that, from geometry, and music, and grammar, and philosophy itself, culling what is useful,* **he guards the faith against assault.**'
> (St Clement of Alexandria, *Stromata*. I.9)

Prominent Christians like Pope John Paul II of the Catholic church, and Saint Augustine of Hippo, and Saint Clement of Alexandria (and countless others), did not believe that there was any conflict between faith and reason. They were two sides of the same coin, two wings of the same bird.

So if faith isn't belief in spite of evidence, then what is it?

If you look up the word faith in the dictionary, the first definition it's likely to give you will probably read something like: 'A strong confidence in a person or thing.' I want you to think about that. If I tell you that I have faith in my teacher, am I trying to say that I believe she exists no matter what? When someone says they have 'faith in' someone or something, it usually means that they trust that person or thing. Having faith in my teacher means that I trust that she is going to keep me safe and teach me things that are true, that sort of thing.

And why do I trust my teacher to do that? Because I know her, and I know that she's qualified to do her job. I would be less likely to trust a stranger I'd never met to teach me, and I'd be even less likely to trust them if I found out they didn't have a teaching degree!

> 'Faith, in the sense in which I am here using the word, is **the art of holding on to things your reason has once accepted, in spite of your changing moods.**'
> (C.S. Lewis, Mere Christianity)

Faith, for the Christian, is anything but blind. We do not have faith in God despite the evidence we see and feel—we have faith in Him because of the evidence we see and feel. This includes our personal experience with God, and how well we know Him. For example, if I'm going through a hard time, but I know that God has gotten me through hard situations before, and I know that He loves me, then I have faith that He will do it again. And that is a perfectly reasonable belief.

On this definition of faith, you can believe in the reality of the Resurrection and still not have faith in God. If you don't know Him (or at least try to know Him), you won't trust Him, and if you don't trust Him, you don't really have faith in Him.

On the other hand, you can still be a perfectly faithful Christian while also using your reason and thinking logically. You can even use your reason to remove barriers that might have hindered your faith. For example, if you really do want to believe that Jesus died and rose for you, and you've experienced Him in your life, but you don't know if the Resurrection could have really been a historical event, that could, very reasonably, make it hard for you to be a Christian. By using your reason to look at the evidence for the Resurrection (as we are doing in this book), it can open the way to a strong faith that agrees with what your reason tells you.

If you see faith and reason like that, then both of them can be ways for you to meet and glorify God. Your mind and your heart are both important to Him.

> *'Jesus said to him, "'You shall love the Lord your God with all your heart, with all your soul, and with all your mind."*
> (Matthew 22:37)

APPENDIX 2: Primary and Secondary Sources:

When you're taking a look at history and evidence, it's really important to understand the difference between a **primary source** and a **secondary source**. It might sound like technical stuff, but it's really a very simple concept.

Let's take a look at a couple of examples to clear up what those terms mean.

Imagine your friend Prim has just bought a gorgeous little puppy. One day, her puppy, being very bored, decides to rip up all his toys!

You weren't there for that event, but Prim saw the dog do it with her own eyes. When she tells you about it, she's a **primary source** of information about that event, because she herself was there and saw it happen.

But imagine that Prim doesn't tell you what happened. Instead, she tells your mutual friend, Sec. Sec, being a bit of a gossip, decides to tell you what Prim told him. Since Sec wasn't there himself, but is getting his information from someone who was there, that makes him a **secondary source** of information about that event.

So in summary, a **primary source** is someone who witnessed the event themselves. In the case of, for example, Christ's appearances after His death, the writings of Matthew are a primary source because he himself saw Jesus after His death.

A **secondary source** is someone who wasn't there themselves, but is getting their information from someone who was (that is, a primary source). An example of this might be Paul's writings about Christ's appearance to the crowd of five hundred people after His death. Paul himself wasn't there to see it, but he'd spoken to people who were there (primary sources), who gave him that information.

APPENDIX 3: HISTORICAL SIGNIFICANCE OF 1 CORINTHIANS 15

> '³ *For I delivered to you first of all that which I also received:* that Christ died for our sins according to the Scriptures, ⁴ and that He was buried, and that He rose again the third day according to the Scriptures, ⁵ and that He was seen by Cephas, then by the twelve. ⁶ After that He was seen by over five hundred brethren at once, of whom the greater part remain to the present, but some have fallen asleep. ⁷ After that He was seen by James, then by all the apostles. ⁸ Then last of all He was seen by me also, as by one born out of due time.'
> (1 Corinthians 15:3-8)

1 Corinthians 15 is, historically, an incredibly significant text. We've already mentioned that it provides a strong testimony for the appearances of Jesus after His death, which is also important because the author, Paul, was originally an enemy of the Christians. But what really makes it interesting is when it was written and where Paul is getting his information from.

Notice that, at the beginning of that passage, Paul specifically says: '*I delivered to you first of all that which I also received*'. This is kind of technical language suggesting that what he's about to say isn't something he himself has made up, but something that has been passed down to him from others. More precisely, what he's about to say is a creed which captures the beliefs of the Christians—mostly likely an oral creed which was already circulating around the early Church.

There are a few other reasons to believe that what he is stating is a creed. Here are just three more:

1. The style of the text itself indicates it's a creed.
2. Paul uses the name Cephas instead of Peter. Cephas is Peter's Aramaic name, and the fact that the original text uses Aramaic (instead of, say, Greek) suggests that it was written very early on.

3. Paul uses phrases like 'the twelve' and 'the third day' which are considered quite primitive, against suggesting that it was written quite early.

So, why is this so important? Take a look at this timeline, and you should see why:

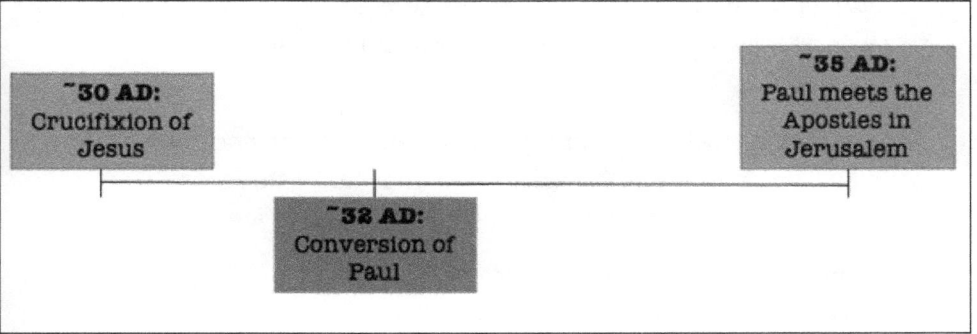

At some point while he was in Jerusalem with the Apostles, Paul would have been given this creed (the one in 1 Corinthians 15 which talks about the Resurrected Christ). Since it's a creed, a sort of formula to capture existing beliefs, it must have existed at least for a little while before it was given to him. That means that the belief that Jesus rose from the dead can be dated within about five years after it actually happened!

Five or so years might sound like a long time to you, but in historical terms, that's basically saying it happened yesterday! This means that belief in the Resurrection could not have been a legend gone wild several generations after the event would've occurred, there was no time for that. This is very clear evidence that the Christians believed that Jesus had risen from the dead pretty much as soon as the event happened.

> 'Paul probably received this report from Peter and James while visiting Jerusalem within a few years of his conversion. The vast majority of critical scholars who answer the question place Paul's reception of this material in the mid-30s CE. Even more sceptical scholars generally agree.'
>
> Habermas (2005) p. 142

For contrast, let's take a look at another famous historical event that very few—if any historians—would doubt actually happened: the assassination of Julius Caesar.

As a refresher Julius Caesar was a Roman Emperor who, history tells us, was assassinated by a bunch of senators on March 15, 44 BC (very specific, I know). Rome was the powerhouse of the Western world at the time, so this was a really big deal—in fact, you probably still study Caesar's death in school!

So, you'd think with an event so important, lots of ancient historians would've written about it, right? Well they did—there are five main sources about Caesar's death and the conspiracy that led up to it:

1. Appian (95-165 AD)—*The Civil Wars*
2. Cassius Dio (163-235 AD)—*History of Rome*
3. **Nicolaus of Damascus** (64-4 BC)—*Life of Caesar Augustus*
4. Plutarch (45–120 AD)—*Lives*
5. Suetonius (69-122 AD)—*Lives*

Notice anything weird about these sources? Except for Nicolaus of Damascus, all of these authors were born at least a century after Caesar's death! They wrote their historical accounts at least a hundred years after the event is supposed to have occurred! And even Nicolaus's account (*Life of Caesar Augustus*) was likely written around 14 BC, which is still three decades after Caesar's actual death! And again, by historical standards, that's actually not that long!

By comparison, the five or so years after the Resurrection doesn't sound like very long, does it? Despite the fact that accounts of Caesar's assassination were written quite a while after the event itself, no self-respecting historian genuinely doubts that Caesar was assassinated.

So, if we are to take a historical perspective on the Resurrection, the texts that detail it are remarkably valuable and almost certainly prove that very, very early on, people believed that Jesus really did rise from the dead.

Further Reading and References

Craig, William (2010). On Guard. Colorado Springs, CO: DavidCCook.

Wishart, Ian (2009). The Jesus Myth: Is Christianity's central story borrowed from older legends?

Retief FP, Cilliers L (December 2003). "The history and pathology of crucifixion". South African Medical Journal. 93 (12)

Berlow, Rustin. (1986). On the Physical Death of Jesus Christ. JAMA. 255. 2753-2753. 10.1001/jama.1986.03370200054011.

Berzon, Todd. Historical Context for the New Testament. https://www.college.columbia.edu/core/content/new-testament/context

Nelson, Thomas (2008). The Orthodox Study Bible. Athanasius Academy of Orthodox Theology, Elk Grove, California. Nashville.

Robinson, Armitage. The Gospel of Peter. http://www.documentacatholicaomnia.eu/01p/0033-0067,_SS_Petrus,_The_Gospel_[Apocryphum]_[Schaff],_EN.pdf

Foster, P. (2007). The Gospel of Peter. The Expository Times, 118(7), 318–325. https://doi.org/10.1177/0014524607077127

Translated by George Prevost and revised by M.B. Riddle. From <u>Nicene and Post-Nicene Fathers, First Series</u>, Vol. 10. Edited by Philip Schaff. (Buffalo, NY: Christian Literature Publishing Co., 1888.) Revised and edited for New Advent by Kevin Knight.<http://www.newadvent.org/fathers/200101.htm>.

Strauss, Barry (2015). The Death of Caesar: The Story of History's Most Famous Assassination. https://erenow.net/biographies/the-death-of-caesar-the-story-of-history-most-famous-assassination/17.php

Strobel, Lee (1998). The Case for Christ: A Journalist's Personal Investigation of the Evidence for Jesus.

N. T. Wright (2003). The Resurrection of the Son of God.

C. S. Lewis (1947). Miracles.

Athanasius On the Incarnation : the Treatise De Incarnatione. Verbi Dei. London :A. R. Mowbray & Co., 1970.

Wallace, Daniel B. (2006). Reinventing Jesus.

Ehrman, Bart (2012). Did Jesus Exist? Huffpost. https://www.huffpost.com/entry/did-jesus-exist_b_1349544

Habermas, Gary R. (2005). Resurrection Research from 1975 to the Present: What are Critical Scholars Saying? Journal for the Study of the Historical Jesus, 3(2), 135–153.

Louth, A. (1987). Early Christian writings: The Apostolic Fathers. Harmondsworth, Middlesex, England: Penguin Books.

Craig, W. L. (2010). On Guard: Defending Your Faith with Reason and Precision. David C Cook.

Retief FP, Cilliers L (December 2003). "The history and pathology of crucifixion". South African Medical Journal. 93 (12): 938–941. PMID 14750495.

C. S. Lewis (1962). They Asked for a Paper: Papers and Addresses.

C. S. Lewis (1952). Mere Christianity.

Pope John Paul II (1998). Fides et Ratio.

Davis, Stephen T. Undated. "Is Belief in the Resurrection Rational? A Response to Michael Martin". http://static1.1.sqspcdn.com/static/f/38692/208874/1263213197257/Is+Belief+in+the+Resurrection+Rational+-+A+Response+to+Michael+Martin.pdf? Accessed December 2015.

Edwards, William D; Gabel, Wesley J; Hosmer, Floyd E. 1986. "On the Physical Death of Jesus Christ". JAMA, 255:1455-1463.

Habermas, Gary R. 2001. "Explaining Away Jesus' Resurrection: the Recent Revival of Hallucination Theories". *Faculty Publications and Presentations (Liberty University)*. Available at http://digitalcommons.liberty.edu/cgi/viewcontent.cgi?article=1106&context=lts_fac_pubs accessed December 2015.

Habermas, Gary R; and Licona, Michael R. 2004. "The Case for the Resurrection of Christ". Kregel.

Joseph, Simon J. 2015. "Redescribing the Resurrection: Beyond the Methodological Impasse?" *Biblical Theology Bulletin,* Volume 45, Number 3, Pages 155–173.

McDowell, J., & Wilson, B. (1993). *Evidence for the Historical Jesus.* Harvest House.

Lexico.com

Talmud, Rosh Hashannah 1.8

St Clement of Alexandria, *Stromata.* I.9

www.ingramcontent.com/pod-product-compliance
Lightning Source LLC
LaVergne TN
LVHW091318080426
835510LV00007B/541